poems for the

Muse Penelope

by

Robert J. Sadler

Volume Ten Chapter Three

Poetic License #4121964

© *rjs 2010*

and other selected poems

cover by
Brian J. Sadler

poems for the
Muse Penelope
and other selected poems

ISBN: 1450573657
EAN-13: 9781450573658

by
Robert J. Sadler
© 2010

robertjsadler.com

wordsculptorpress

10987654321

drawing
his bow
the arrow flies
and a suitor dies
long live
Penelope, Odysseus
& Telemachus
as another arrow flies

and
if you are
confused
'this'
is
for you

3

flaming questions
~for PH

what of the spark that never died
that never became a flame
that never gulped the freshening
oxygen of sustenance
that never had to gasp its last breath

what of the spark that never died
that remains ever potent
in that triad—needing only
air to breathe and flesh to eat;
the mortal flesh of dry kindling

what of the spark that never died
that resides where it never rusts
never consumes itself—waiting
as it burns in the memory
waiting on a future thought

what of the spark that never died
 …will it purposefully set alight
its surroundings or spontaneously
combust or—like a careless
moment's tossed match
     —become a raging forest fire

NH-NH-NH
~for PH

seven years
captive to Calypso
another year under the witching
gaze of the goddess Circe
I have been ship-wrecked by Poseidon
have strained at my lashings
to hear the sweet Sirens' song
—escaped the many-headed Scylla
and the whirlpool of Charybdis
        if only in the dreams
of dreaming myself home

if I may
I will dream tonight
of Penelope
who slumbers near enough
to smell the ocean's breath
and far enough away
to sleep within the borders
of New Hampshire's
winter stand of frozen waterfalls
& forests of slim white birches
anchoring heavy snows

I will dream tonight
of Penelope
asleep in a house old enough
to sing and sigh with shifts
in the pressing winds of night
old enough to have lace curtains
and candles in its windows
not old enough or near enough

to Ithaca to [come springtime]
have suitors upon the lawns
as Odysseus winds
his way home

Freesia
~for PH

while you sleep
in the spider's spin of a gossamer dream
and time trembles unaware
the tendrils of connection are drawn
closer—more near

held by the epoxy of memory
as if iridaceous bulbs
waiting on the winter's thaw
and a spring's warmth
to arise

Questions for Penelope
~for PH

what mysteries could I solve
that would turn your head
what words could I speak
that would enchant your soul

are there thoughts you've never thought
that I could entice you to consider
are there places you have never been
that we could visit holding hands

what pictures could we take
that would not look like those
taken with the dozen others
who have held our hands

if I whispered in your ear
would you prefer the left or right
do you drink coffee late at night
or only with your breakfast

do lipstick kisses adorn
your coffee cup
regardless of the time of day
and what's your favorite shade

do your nails match your lips
or do you prefer the natural look
do you have any tattoos
if you could choose a middle name

whose would you use—
isn't it amazing we still have
questions that four decades
have yet to answer

Answers for Penelope
~for PH

even if you don't keep your heart
locked, keep the key handy
I may be a dream-maker
but I do not possess
a Fairy Godmother's magic wand
to make them come true

just acting on impulse, instinct
and a connectedness I didn't expect
you are safe, but not too safe
from the wheres my fictive mind
strays for all those reasons it does
—hoping not to pay the piper

for the moment let me trifle lightly
with your heart as you mystify mine
in this who-knows world
where years of wondering, like water,
seeks its own level
is it a hill we climb or descend
I know not—all I know is that a stream
runs along side us murmuring *stop*
take a drink, don't gulp, sip slowly

should we stop, keep walking or run
to a destination of unknown making
which upon arrival we might sadly say
oh, we've been here before & turn
                                    away
to take refuge in the before—before

9

a heart can't press reverse
~for PH

like a cat in a high bough caught
my heart shivers—not knowing
how many lives it has left

can it withstand the night's wind
tomorrow's rain or snow
or the rocks the neighbor kid throws

will it loose its grip when
the fireman on his long ladder
reaches out to save it

everyone watching, knowing
and wondering if it could creep
out to the limb's outer limit

why can't it just turn around
grin like its Cheshire twin
and climb safely down

Alice In Wonderlanding
~for PH

have I just convinced myself
that there is no counsel
for going where
we've counseled ourselves
                         not to go
is there no flame I am not
willing to test against my hand
—a voice says such hurts heal
another voice shakes it head
knowing you don't heal so fast
                          anymore

when you can't trust yourself
all that is left is the guidance
of unseen hands to pull at yours
before—the flame takes its bite
before emotion's whirlpool
pulls you into its vortex…
          and where *does* that
      rabbit hole lead, Alice

bringing me a smile
~for PH

you
think *you* must write
something
that would bring
a smile to *my* face
          tonight
don't you know you have
already done that
each time you have written
—oh, you don't know that?

I know the smile of fun
      the feel of laughter
that jiggles and giggles
inside you
that like the tree alone
      falling in the forest
          no one hears
but is well and truly there

you have all the qualities
of a Muse, a goddess
          without guile
who pities not the piteous
who fashions her duties
as pre-ordained
shouldered with a grace
unaware of those
who gather the smallest
of moon beams
that radiate from her
      as if grains of sand
          slipping
    from her sandals
      as she walks
to make simple poems
from her light.

pay no attention to the man
behind the curtain
~for PH

shhhhhhh, be not frightened
by the *words* of the enchanted
they cannot help themselves
it is only a spell
                    [it can be broken]
enjoy them
as if a series of sunrises
as if they possess a beauty
worthy of the moment

they are not a mirror
you cannot enchant yourself
unless you hold them up
and look
too deeply into their syntax
or question the morphology
                    of their metaphors

these words can be forgotten
as easily as midnight dismisses
a sunset as meaningless
or disregarded as
if a grasshopper fiddling above
                    a winter's ant hill

shhhhhhh, be not frightened
by the *words* of the enchanted
their warmth is short-lived—
they cannot: shake your hand;
hug you; kiss your lips; or
                    whisper in your ear

when she said hello
there was no goodbye in her voice
~for PH

I was
as compact and composed
as an old can of coffee before
it is opened and that great
rush of coffee-smell escapes
its vacuumed pressure

the phone rang and
out poured a voice like bells
my ears have not stopped
ringing nor my heart singing
but that *pwooosh*
has gone out of me
like a balloon released
propelled around the room
and yet I cannot stand
I must sit in reverent reverie
waiting for the adrenaline
to dissipate

you have no idea
what you have done to *me*
from hello
to our proffered
yet insincere goodbyes
that meant
        at most
till later—when soon
      becomes now…
and when she said goodbye
—in her voice *I* heard only
               hellos

girl with the ruby red slippers
~for PH

with sufficient muscle
and strength of grasp most anything
can be held
        but hold it too tightly
           and it might die
and the only muscle
that can never be held is the heart
no matter how hard we try

it's best to let it flutter
in your open hands
like a queenly Monarch
and let her choose whether to stay
              or fly

the strongest hold I know
is the strength to let you go
and the joy of having you prefer
           to stay
         not fly away

if I have the temerity
[I call it grace] to remind you
from time to time
        where your slippers are
it is only my way of suggesting
the possibilities on the other side
of the rainbow—
of relaxing my grip
of honoring your free will

therefore I hold you in the open
hands of the deepening affection
the common words for which
should be spoken
face to face, ear to ear…

15

the day the petals fell
~for PH

it was an ordinary day
the weather was cold and crisp
new snow lay on old—
neither caring
they had already done their work
        the day the petals fell

they fluttered down like curtains
of flowered snowflakes
        only larger and softer
gathering around her feet
as her blood rushed to greet them
soon in joy they rose
first to cover her shins—dry
and powdery against her skin

as if a potion they proclaimed
their power, claimed her thoughts
assuaged her heart, held her fast
in their silky embrace—
and when she finally moved
they swirled gently about her
        kissing at her knees
        the day the petals fell

a dream, a thought, an intention
like focused desire they surrounded
—an outward manifestation
that matched her swelling feelings
each petal a moment's passion
lying dormant waiting to be stirred
walked through, run through

pirouetting in emotions she turned
and turned, surrounded
        by her thoughts
of love and its perfect slumbers
she let them lead her and take her
        the day the petals fell

why we wish upon a star
~for PH

that which can be recalled
is here as if yesterday were now
that which can be imagined can be seen
forming root by limb by limb by leaf
that which can be felt can be manifest
when sufficient todays
                              become tomorrow

the law of attraction *they say*
is always at our beck and call—waiting
yearning for the lock to find its key
listening for the calling words
beckoning wish & desire from might-be
into what is to-be [with adequate want]
                              into the thing that is-now

some dreams
~for PH

some dreams we are not meant to see
they remain occluded in subconscious
libraries where all our dreams
meet to tell stories, swap tales
   they know each other, those secret
dreams—the faint brothers and sisters
of our remembered imaginings
which we try to claim upon waking
—remembering a quick but elusive
thought, a certain smell, a warmth,
a taste of lips
for which the conscious mind reaches
trying to gain purchase
                but never quiet grasps
as the strength of *now* overpowers
a night's *then* of dreams

this I was told [by The Maker of Dreams
as I caught him in mid-step, stepping
off the dock—in that one instant
between sleep and not] that *whatsoever*
thought your breath breathes, becomes
a ship forever sailing your sea of dreams

and he assured me *even if you thought*
you dreamed naught of her
she is there if she inhabits your breath
…sleep came as I breathed out: Penelope
then sipped your name back inside of me

the Ferris wheel
~for PH

what is perception
but a Ferris wheel going going round
and round, never going up or down
only riders on it radians
in their own time and space feel
the tug and release of gravity

the wheel is a wheel whether
it moves or not—turning
is not its only axial
purpose
experience is its function
—the leaving behind
of worthy imagination for the tang
of feeling the earth move
when the earth is a mere observer

we are merely the riders, the actors,
                    the livers of our dreams
lovers of the mystical union
in search of reality
where
        perception is often seduced
by the majesty of verisimilitude

[—yes the earth moves
as we move upon it like a sunbeam
dispelling darkness, like you
                    upon my heart
displacing melancholia with desire]

it is reality for which anticipation
prepares us in all its lugubrious lack
of haste… it is on what I wait
—the reaching through the veil
to touch the beating heart of love

19

would you be jealous
of the thousand children I've had
before I met you

poems are children, you know,
and equally loved
and some the favored few

the poet's words
~for PH

before now
I have written of many things:
coffee cups and kisses
target's hits and misses
Asian dancers, war, Aprils
and Octobers—of love
and the ladies of my nights
—everything but you
—all before is old
—everything now is new

would you have me put
the paper of my poems
to the flame of past fires
and let them thus consume
or bear the burden of a past
knowing yesterday's sunset
                cannot affect
        the sunrise of our days
and thus let those sunsets live
their death sequestered,
        a simple poem on a page

Act One
~for PH

You act on me
as if a magnet
pulling me nearer to you...
me hungering for that moment's
                    first touch
hungering for your sustenance
though neither proximity
                nor provisions are in sight
…how can it be that I have more to say
than I've ever said before
how can it be that you desire to hear
what to each of us is so new
how can it be that
                your laughter thrills me so
                or the thought that one day
        I might hold you while you laugh
                or even whisper my name
                is so earnestly desired

re/connection
~for PH

here and there
so near the ocean
so far from my arms
sheltered—in my heart

lost like a tree in a forest
once on it's edge—
deep within its borders
generations surround it now
those feelings are flooding
back—being the tree
not just part of the forest
as a singular worthiness
—I can see you now
always always always there
our roots growing closer
infatuation is love's
anticipation

sheltered—in my heart
so far from my arms
so near the ocean
there and here

this
~for PH

this.....
must be something very special
perhaps it is like a sublime binomial
distribution, coefficient; an equation
yet to be dreamed
for whatever *this* is that we share
[whatever ineffable feeling
this is] must never have been felt
before
            for there seems no words
that express, encircle, ensnare
capture or contain what we know
is manifest between us
                and if *this* had happened
                somewhere in the world
                to some other someones
                they would already have
                named *this*
some might miss-name *this* as
love—but we would say, no
this is something
more

Predicates
~for PH

Our *this-ness* requires no understanding
it is what we have manifested
within each other

It only requires sustenance, the bread
and butter of joy and anticipation
the simple burning of calories

It has no end unless an end is sought
and diminishes only when chased
as the Acadians found

As a sun reclining atop a hill
is no longer there once the hill is topped
but rests where it always was, out of reach

Our challenge is to not allow *this* to slip
beyond our grasp nor predict
its place tomorrow

Our charge is to bask
in *this* today as if it were our last
with the grace to let tomorrow surround us

Angels, Deer, & Clair de lune
~for PH & JH [twin snow angels]

on the
snow, yesterday's angels
we left as etched likenesses
of ourselves
[whose wings
are worn at the edges
by the freshening winds]
are joined this morning
by last nights wandering
scampering tracks
of voles and field mice

the deer did not come this way
last night and must be warming
their bedding spots
           deep in the woods
new snow begins to fall
further softening sounds—
and day-old snow-angels' wings

then fingers touch
caressing keys whose hammers
strike their coiled notes
softly piercing the snowy air
           in alert, a deer lifts
       its head and twitches an ear
toward the nearby home

where a piano issuing forth
the sounds of Clair de lune
turns day into night & winter's
chill into an indolent spring

where the warmth of summer
memories ride the whitening
of a cool silver moon
its touch like a never forgotten
embering heat—your hearts

25

show and tell
~for PH

how could I show you how
　　　　　I feel when I cannot see you
how can I tell you if I can't find the words

as a blind man I desire the gift of sight
of seeing you across some diminishing
distance walking
　　　　　　　even running into my arms
holding you with arms that have practiced
crossing that street tapping, tapping
　　　　　　　　　with my red-tipped cane

though momentarily bereft of vision,
by grace—I found Cupid's quiver of words
　　[more swift than his arrows flying true]
　　　　　　　with which to pierce your heart

to mortally wound
any sense of flight that might gather you
to other errant fields, away from my voice
farther away from my arms
　　　　　　　　　where once seen
　　　　　　　　　you can be shown

swept away in the moonlight
~for PH

your
voice is a tangible embodiment
to the sweet words you write—
your gifts of appreciation
acknowledgement—hearten me
and flatter
and then you sang
a song I love, sang it softly
and sweetly in my ear
it was as if—
          for those moments…
you were in command
of all of heaven's bees
whose gathered nectars
became the treasure I heard
in the moonlight
—it was as if, honey could sing
and you were lovingly drizzling
it over and over me

working late
~for PH

here I am, 3:30 in the a.m.
wide awake and dreaming
of the pleasure
of having you here
to come to bed to

to know that labor's done
and though you found
               sleep
several hours ago—
as I come to bed somehow
your body welcomes me
we fuse
in languorous relaxation
in seductive possession
of the moment
before dreams can dream
the morning
where—for the first time
you realize I am there
with you, and not a dream

to have you reach for me
at that moment
is a drawing-near
that approaches—nirvana

Ferris Wheel [2]

~for PH

I am reduced to suspect speculation
on the probabilities
       of more joy than *this* brings
is it possible that feeling the actual
beat of your heart underhand
            could exceed *this*
would your heart be racing wildly
or would that trembling be my hand

I've just checked my journal,
NASA and the weather channel
confirming that
          the last eighteen days
against all rationale against all odds
exist—did one by one transport me
to the top of a double-Ferris wheel
      I am stopped there—swinging

a future lies out across the horizon
and I can't wait to get down
to follow my shadow east
until the sun comes up in your eyes

dream melodies
~for PH

the quiet moments come—the sounds
of mellow horns play in the background
while unseen fingers quick march
then slowly sashay across the keys
as violins vibrate to a swelling crescendo
all the visuals—real and imagined—flash
before my closed eyes, a miniature screen
fills my internal universe with your face
these stills are animated by your laughter
—those sweet sweet sounds I've heard
leave me wanting what I cannot yet have
the lips I long to kiss
       or watch, blossom—into a smile
            —I sleep
      dreaming melodies of you

as well defined as
a 96 Ct. box of Crayolas®
—with a built-in sharpener
drawing pots of gold...

your voice; a rainbow
~for PH

there is a color to your voice
it is like pink cheeks and blue eyes
it is filled with a sunrise of laughter
and the deep magentas and purples
of a sunset on the mesa that sighs
before the night can kiss it goodbye

there is a brightness to your hello
a wink in your how-do-you-do
a glow in your words that emanates
from the deepest part of you
to think it could be, as you proclaim,
a response to me—can be only magic

there is a softness in your breath
as you breathe—and my name issues
forth... a warmth of tone resembling
a peppery piquant bassoon—that rides
a rumbling heart like kettles drumming
dare I beg to hear those words, so near

drop: seen and unseen
~for PH

mystical, the drop of water falling
its perfect symmetry replicated
bouncing on air above the plane
of its essence—only taking part
tossing its reduction upward to fall
    again
          and again till its nihilness
               is assimilated

with each part ingested a ringwave
emanates outward toward oblivion
or the nearest shore
from which it rebounds sourceward
these recombinant waves
arrive full of their travels
unable to account for themselves
—but you drop a single compliment

that rushes over me like a tidalwave
that carries me as untethered flotsam
away to the far reaches of my being
only to rush back to you—
like the drop I am becoming
          a little less of *me*
just as each drop overcomes gravity
and tension's surface—becoming *we*

Baklava & Peaches
~for PH

It is not that I have never tasted
sugared honey wrapped in pastry;
I have held the delicate baklava
oozing its aphrodisiacs of honey,
pistachio, cardamom and cloves
——my lips have relished its sticky
residue and held its fragile phyllo
inhaled its fragrant spices
as nibble by nibble ecstasy ensued
——as if a eunuch in Sultan's harem
    in charge of the Persian peach

It is that I understand his
only imagining the forbidden
fruit, the smell of its swollen
blossom, texture of its outer leaves
dreaming of his fingers piercing
its fleshy tissues——lifting its juices
to his waiting tongue——letting this
flavor indelibly etch
each taste bud as if chiseled
in the granite of his memory
——knowing just as winter
holds the spring
    this sweet, remains out of reach

only time & distance
~for PH

one phase one phrase remains
hidden from our speech, cloaked
in the conventions of imagined
memories and the touch of reality

we bloody our tongues
holding back from confessions
that seem so near confessing
from the pure torture of separation

for though my lips and your ear
are near—they are connected
by the merest thread of sound
via telephonic Furies

it is only to your face, my arms
surrounding you, that the truth
of my professions should find
and mark your heart

Ah, Furies...
~for PH

Alecto cease your search
Megaera begrudge me not and Tisiphone
I have yet to commit the crimes for which
you fly the earth to avenge

I speak not Greek, and know not
sussuarances—placating prayers to which
you might me hear
beyond the walls of your temple palace

Daunt me not as I seek
the shores of the Muse Penelope
to place my head upon the breast
of her altar and plead my troth

From Tulsa to Tulsa
~for PH

As Ærhoden learned, 'it's all circular'
that point from which we start
and [though as tortured as Ulysses'
path] to which we eventually return

It is as if all the Sirens and Cyclops
and the gentle guile of Circe's beauty
was only a godly literary device
to keep me from you

But it is to you Penelope
that I return—a battered and better
man than the one you last knew
a wiser man more grateful to be home

flying
~for PH

oh the mysteries
of the yet to be known
places sans a map to mark
the spot Fate waits to be shown

are there vistas high, mountains
to be caressed as if a mother's breast
and valleys to be explored
to the trilling heart of their depth

are there skies in which to float
amused at lesser bees and birds
who must still use wings to fly
to reach their ecstasy

Shakespeare's Macbeth, Act V, Scene V
—*Dunsinane. Within the Castle.*

To-morrow, and to-morrow, and to-morrow
Creeps in this petty pace from day to day,
To the last syllable of recorded time;

What of when? The Muse asks.
~for PH

you ask how long till spring
how long till the long-awaited no longer waits
is it only a matter of sunrises in a sequence
that though unfathomable can be counted

the answer lies in tomorrow
that most ineffable of days that belongs
not to history nor to the moment
when the sounds of love find your ears

spring cannot be foretold in futurity
beyond the existential nature of hope
where the seed of seasons past
is reborn as the ripened fruit of now

and now is still a then
a yet to be a phantasmal allegiance
of what we hope to hold
and our grasp can then contain

you ask how long till spring
how long till the long-awaited no longer waits
it is but one yesterday away
when *this* tomorrow dawns

37

Shakespeare's Cymbeline, Act IV, Scene III
—*A Room In Cymbeline's Palace.*

All other doubts, by time let them be clear'd;
Fortune brings in some boats that are not steer'd.

by time let them be clear'd
~*for PH*

the banner has been raised, it flutters
in the winds the spoken sacred words
have turned from distant hills
to fill the flags of now

gently caressing your
cheeks with the blush of spring
and the rush of excitations freely felt
in the arms of he who feels the same

not to worry
~*for PH*

there is no malefaction
in the ointment of time
it is an easy salve to apply
it is the resultant healing
for which we pine
and quickness
            is not its virtue
though once healed
the wound's passing seems
the sooner than memory
can calculate—
the
    rift
between yesterday
and tomorrow will soon
be nursed back to health
with a single kiss
upon the brow of now

noun, not a verb transitive
~for PH

in the deepness of night
where the only light I see

is in your eyes
those sparkling orbs
from which so much
of you is sensed and senses
that they might tightly close
in preparation
for that which only the music
of your voice gives notice
though the body agrees
would be a moment
when such words
as previously
spoken

find their meaning—as if they
had never needed to be spoken

supraliminal utterances
~for PH

you give my words their power
it is you my Muse
that inspires them, they reflect
you more than me

if they 'make' you tremble
it is you desiring thus to move
were you a mountain
and my words commanded you
and you moved, that indeed
would be testimony of their power

were that true
you would already be in my arms

39

the days of its shadows
~for PH

and though it is not upon
my command or yours that we wait
it is on Time
whose ear gives us no audience

it is on Time
that blind institution of man
demarcating here from there
and every shadow of in between

it is in the completion of the words
we wait signing *three blind mice*
playing *blind man's bluff* [oh God]
the nursery rhymes I find in you

the days of its shadows
will pass, the sun will surround us
with a living moment written
to the 'disk'—ceaseless

it is on Time
we wait as we have always,
                if impatiently, waited
                for its secret fullness

roots of a dream
~for PH

I may have wasted yesterday, last hour
or the last second
what I cannot waste is the next

second
minute
hour
or
day

—much less a single solitary tomorrow

yet it is that tomorrow or series of them
for which we wait, upon which we hope
indeed dream
    [yes tomorrow is a dream, Gibran]
and yesterday is today's remembrance
—a facile memory in a too easy world
of want
    and yet want is a powerful brother
        to his sister desire
orphans, luxuriating in a futuristic home

yet it is in future's home I seek asylum
bereft of memory's yesterday
sequestered from this transient moment
for it has passed and passed and passed
again before before could become now

my conundrum—I must have waited for
this moment, when it and you were still
    a dream
and yet you are oh so near and oh so far
so real—that dreaming imagined kisses
    have a taste
too hard to describe now, but are plainly
defined in the frequent fantasies
    of a world
    composed of
needing and wanting and waiting for you

Missing You
~for PH

The blue river mountain, the golden
Aspen leaf, the dance of thistle down
as spring arrives and the cattle
return to the valley

Are cherished rights of passage
from frozen streams to greening
hay meadows—it is winter now
coffee on the fire

It percolates among the loneliness
of seasons of desire unfulfilled
a cabin cool in summer, fire-warmth
to stave the chill, not the lonely hearth

What he misses most is that golden
haired girl with her blue-river eyes
whose laughter, like the thistle down,
brings spring into his heart

before daybreak
~for PH

It seemed a short night
when I awoke earlier with thoughts
of you twizzling in my mind and...
the scent of your hair lingering
in the imagined air

I reached to gather you into my arms
found another day had begun
without the breath of your voice
in my ear or the heat of your body
to awaken *this* awakening

42

hands free
~for PH

who would have thought
a bicycle was a hands-free device
—except to those who can pedal
fast enough to keep the wheels straight

but there are jobs were hands are handy
jumpin' freight trains surely takes two
the same for boxers and drummers
and rowers in one-man sculls

bull riders keep one hand on the rope
the other waves to the crowd for balance
while the bully says com'on I've one hand
tied behind my back, just to make it fair

society warns us to keep both hands
on the wheel but look at you, Girl—your
hands in the air—who would've thought
that poetry was a hands-free device

Carole King
I feel the earth move
from *Tapestry*

I feel the earth move under my feet
I feel the sky tumblin' down
I feel my heart start to tremblin'
whenever you're around
—ooh Baby

moving
~for PH

ensconced in the warmth of blankets
piled high against the New England
winter [where even the cat
        likes to sleep on a heating pad]
recumbent in the cocoon of weariness
fires banked against the January snow
you listen to the low, warm, murmurs
of poetry in the air

abed, waiting in a warmth of words
that stirs you and keeps sleep at bay
you listen as they, within you, play
strings and chords you thought long
since lost—letting the words sing
to you—experiencing them
their vibration enough
                    to give them voice

44

fireside chat
~for PH

the fire warms the walls against the chill
of snow beyond the window's cold pane
you sit reading words I've written
as if, they speak to you
as if, you knew what I was thinking
        the small bright difference
in the specific yet malleable meaning
of words encoded for other's eyes
and yet decoded by your ears

in
my yarn-spinning, the blanket of woolen
words you wear
        are meant to keep you warm
          as if a dram of fine liqueur
            from the inside out
are meant to vouchsafe your heart—until
we can touch, what has not been touched
        my lips to your ear
a-buzz with words we both hold, so dear

undeniable
~for PH

what is deep inside, somewhere within the depth
of the heart—both the one that beats faster
at the sound of your voice
and the heart wherein resides the holiest of emotions
that most reverent of meaning between beings
both divine and human
> of the former it is known, a given
>> in faith & grace
> of the latter, it is waited on with a
> testing of our limitations
> of knowledge
> of history
> of experience

regardless of experience, of history, it is the knowing
which takes precedence
for when one knows the truth and still denies it
such is the root of foolishness; I, my love, am no fool

many an old saying is apt, perhaps none is more so
than: *the truth will out*—I apologize for holding back
—for asking you, to withhold from you, the pleasure
of letting your heart speak, and apologize
for breaking my own self-imposed dictum—to wait
until I could hold your face in my hands
look into your eyes and tell
you… as tonight, with my heart flowing
outward, reaching for yours in faith & grace—when
> tonight, I told you I love you

guest room
~for PH

as if a secret cloister the guest room
provides us the privacy
to give voice to your thoughts
let our laughter out to run around
the room like misbehaving children
and to cloak the sighs and whispers
that seem to others, out of place
                    so late at night

as if a secret cloister the guest room
provides us the privacy
of a confessional—sans the priest
for we have confessed and confessed
time and again a shopping list
                    of desires
& breathless await the other to assign
the appropriate penance

as if a secret cloister the guest room
is our telephonic trysting place
our words no longer singing
along the cross-country miles of wires
and poles but bouncing off sky-dishes
[as the fork runs away with the spoon]
you there, me here—
                    hearing each other swoon

the unfinished when
~for PH

nothing will seem close until close is you
in my arms—time will not move faster as
another tomorrow dawns and another day
lays between, as if a good but unwelcome
friend—you want them there
      till you are ready for them to leave

all the measures of time and distance are
just that, markers from here to there—
frustrating, when all you want is to have
there be here, now
                now is not two weeks
                   or ten days away

not even when tomorrow is the last day
not even when your plane is in the air
nor will it be now
  when I am driving to the airport—no
not until my eyes see yours, the smile
upon your lips, and I can finally—feel
the tremble of your heart against mine

when the phone call ends
~for PH

there is the moment, more an instant,
right after you say 'goodnight my dear'
and before your sprite's voice disappears
that all the world seems right and real

then that cellular connection is broken
and the room around me dims
and the smile your joy traced on my lips
becomes a tight lingering line of anxiety

you only know the depth of your desire
it is mine you enquire of when speaking
frankly of yours—and mine, I know
and will not tell, but in time will show

wandering the internal mews of loneliness
chanting your name I slowly find my way
to bed—your warmth only imaginary
and tomorrow the next thing I know
              —as I wait for your next hello

holding joy
~for PH

perhaps I am most thrilled
at the prospect of, in just a few days,
drawing you into the circumference
             of my warm embrace

letting the circle of my arms tighten
around your waist and pull you near
the power of your smile filling the air
            and my arms holding joy

the fall
~for PH

does love fall like a foolish snowflake
drifting with the slightest breeze
on its crenellated edges, its surface rife
with air between its crystalline spokes

doesn't it dance through the air
and wait its turn to reach the ground
only to touch down in soft communion
with all those fools that fell before

or does it race through the skies
       like an exhausted balloon
who has run out of breath
only to plunge spent, into a heap

does love fall like a dying ember
a pop of a spark
lighting the moment with its heat
then drop—a cold dark piece of char

or does it run to the edge of tomorrow
that endless abyss and dive
toward whatever darkness or light
lives in the arms of such gravity

does love grow like a spring bud
slowly but inexorably toward the sun
drinking of cloud-waters, its roots
supping on the Earth's mineral stew

doesn't love always—just blossom
when the elements properly align
or does it sometimes explode into being
on the peerless touch of a lightening bolt

yes it is both, it is all—yes it is you
yes it is a fall with no up, no down
yes it is as simple as a quickening
into the slow adamantine now of *this*

Penelope's Secret
~for PH

from store dressing room to boudoir
the ensemble is unpacked, unwrapped
unfolded, smoothed and admired—
some pieces hung on the back of a door
watching how they appear in the changing
light—as you study them some more

a wondering takes you
how does it feel—you ask—followed
by a clandestine session of dress-up
and close mirrored-inspection
augmented with fantasies
of how in the syncopated ups and downs

of a Merry-Go-Round wind
how your hair & your gossamer garment
float slow-motion in the gathering air
as you ride your leisurely loping pony
to the music of the calliope's next crescendo
and smile a secret smile—a twin-smile

M. of M.M.
for PH

into the hands of all rest the gifts
of which only a few take advantage
—gifts we see in others, not ourselves

among these are the gifts of insight
and inspiration each in their own way heal
evoking this spirit is in what we write

writers, other artists, singers and musicians
see this healing though to some it is cloaked
in a mystery they fail to understand

is it so different then to realize—that healing
which is at the heart of art can be accessed
by the artist for its own sake

that the Great Giver of Gifts
allows us to enter into what to us appears
as coincidence, as magic, as miracle

when it is only directing
that which we are given to the benefit
of another; Spirit, to spirit to spirit

whether it is the evoking of emotion
the healing salve of love
or the magic of mitigating a migraine

from *Shakespeare in Love*—
In the grip of Fennyman's henchmen:

Henslowe: *Allow me to explain to you about the theater business.*
           The natural condition is one of insurmountable obstacles
           on the road to imminent disaster.

Fennyman: *So what do we do?*

Henslowe: *Nothing—strangely enough it all turns out well.*

Fennyman: *How?*

Henslowe: *I don't know; it's a mystery.*

Shakespeare in Love: **Deleted Scene**
~for PH

last night did you not wonder
if the sun would still be here today
did not years of seeing sunrises
convince you of the probabilities
did a single day or two of clouds
give you pause
        to examine your expectation

and yet you ran to the post
out through the drifts of fresh snow
the wind tearing at your anticipation
hoping there would be a letter
and tearing it open you read:
I am absolutely DELIGHTED
        to hear from you

and then the clouds flew away
as if expertly pulled by the unseen
craft of celestial stagehands
the solar spotlight shines
and you step to center stage to sing:
Where O Where
        Is My Poem Today

53

lightning's strike
~for PH

with the eyes of pain I looked
neither deep nor far
nor upon a far fair shore
my ship
a-sail in timorous waters
that turn to gale
on Poseidon's rough breath
carried as if a soul wandering
lost
    bereft of sustenance
         starved of passion

days and days and years
passed
without the single fire
upon whose hearth is warmed
my own cool heart
         only to stand afield
listening to the thunder's peal
as luck and fate and God
[as if Thor and Cupid combined
their magi's craft]
and threw from heaven
one lightning-bolted-arrow
of love—that pierced my heart

& as my melancholia lay dying
the fruits of love's labors found
revived in me such joys as
happiness, smiles and laughter
—still weak from a previous
sadness that *this* arrow now heals
you strengthen my sight
to reveal on this arrow's shaft
the name of my love
            Penelope

with words *this* is formed
~for PH

words are spirit and from them form
the creations we creatures speak
and sing and write
that most single power of conveyance
whose idea feels the swell of hearts
that yearn and spoil for love
is but a pen or key stroke from your
eyes and then to your ears
the words I whisper
they are simple words spoken often
perhaps in jest or as a parrot
repeated without weight
yet these same words I speak to you
are blessed with powers
to wholly heal
life long left intentionally untended
with my inner most breath
I write I love you

in baklava hidden
~for PH

within baked layers of flaky *phyllo* dough
the unseen ingredients wait—their delight
appreciated with each bite; your voice
the honey, your laughter the spice
each wrapped in layers of memory
that hide just below what is seen and heard
playing as if constant background music
to my every subconscious thought
a flavor, a moment must be tasted
to be appreciated—logistics, materiel,
and place give parameters—yet blossomed
buds of taste are our only arbiters
as experience teaches
and refines our likes and dislikes
but this is a blind taste test of a delicacy
so exquisitely described in sound & words
that I happily wait in unfeigned anxiety
for you to grace my lips with reality

setting sail
~for PH

in certainty I wait
one more day for years and weeks
and months to end in the twinkling
of your eyes—silently spoken
by the smile on your face
and warmth of your embrace

I long to kiss and caress
your every dimension when silence
is no longer spoken—to hear
the metes and bounds of your breath
its rhythms its poetry, the drumming
of your heart as it murmurs *now*

and *again*—when our voyage
of words can weigh anchor with full
sail, calling them each by name:
main, jib, mizzen, topsail; spreading
them to the wind, tacking into deep
waters for the pure love of sailing

Valentine Dreams
~for PH

from the cloud of sleep I wake
in dreams of you
as if a frozen fog, their memories
cling to me, at first cold & crystalline
clear, only to melt in a mist—a film
of what was and is harder and harder
to remember—
except—that the smile you smiled
is like a kiss, now upon my waking
face, its joy lingering like crumbs
of a favorite dessert
waiting on a fevered tongue tip's
careful swipe—so nothing's missed

and other selected poems

4203 Gilbert Avenue

as if
that's all there is to do
he watches the rain
melt the dusty waterspots
from his window
as tonight's evening rain
grows

a few cigarettes
of standing there
blankly staring through the panes
he heaves a few well-earned sighs
        [this usually cures his
        self-imposed insomnia
          but not tonight]

seems
he needs to be close to something
the street corner's too far away
and the street light
is standing too forlornly alone
        to be much a friend

while looking out the window
at the rain
he's been lending support to the wall
   strange how walls
      will warm to you
         if you lend them
         your shoulder for a while

Gilbert Avenue Observatory

from the balcony
watching jet-stream cirrus clouds
he noticed
the
trees began
              again today
         to loose their leaves

looks to be the makings
         of another leafless fall

sounds of silence

lay quietly
hear soft breathing
feel her soft skin
still moist and warm
the after-touch feels so good

awareness comes again
the stereo plays its sounds of silence
next to us the open window comes alive
being watered by the gentle soaking rain
all tenseness gone and relaxed

a rain-cooled breeze
        rolls across my back and legs
I feel her shiver next to me
her arm encircles and draws me near
I turn to catch a knowing smile
our mingling thoughts merge

my mind moves-more-quickly-now
I want to stay, but I say
        I must go
                rain or no
she turns away to hide her tears
in the darkness
five minutes more
    all right,
            I will stay a little longer

I raise the sheet to keep the cool off
hands behind my neck I think
the rain
        will it never cease
she falls asleep tired but sanguine
her needs filled she sleeps and smiles

worries now begin
thoughts alone
      though she is near
wonder what tomorrow
sans the rain will bring
does the sun really melt love like butter

in the daytime she longs for me and the night
at night
      she wants me all through the night
I am man and mortal be
this flesh that surrounds my heart and soul
methinks the lady doth not protest enough

laugh as much as complain
who coaxes who would be hard to say
she would be hurt if I said so
      I like her hair the other way
but tomorrow is soon

another cigarette
the rain is losing strength
pink streaks cloud the sky
I am sleepy now
will she want me when she wakes
      and finds me sleeping

lay quietly
hear soft breathing
mine now matching hers
awareness comes and goes
      awareness comes and ....

CASA TERRON

from
the balcony
we watched the sun
so long in the sky
fall
   toward that jut
   of hills that
   frames the bay
crimson-ing
the clouds
like the spectrums
of a color wheel
as
      it
         fell

with
the colors
draining
from that canvas
of sea and sky
the hills began
to catch-light
in a fire
of electricity

seventy-five
and
100 watt diamonds
massed-together
strung-together
   pearl-like
or sprinkled sparsely
here   and
      there
outlined and bedazzled
the night
surrounding
Acapulco Bay

across its mouth
the breezes tropical
floated toward our shore
on slippery shouldered
ocean waves
     hit the beach
          and
stumbled out of the surf
soaked
in sea-smells

climbing
rock by tree
the breezes
freshened up
the hillside
gathering the
perfumed scents
of almond
and hibiscus
along the way

crossing
calle Buenavista
las brisas
flowed lugubriously
through
Casa Terron

where
first-night
guests
still adjusting
to its serenity
sip
after-dinner coffee
after-dinner drinks

and
relax
while sharing
those quiet moments
before
the night sounds
now politely passive
began to shout
for attention

sleepy eyes
staring into
the deep darkness
of jungle recesses
only
a leopard's leap
away
are
startled
as iguana
trumble through
the undergrowth

and
chameleons
in need of pedicures
click-clack
        and scutter
across marble floors
and up spot-lighted
white stuccoe'd walls

to
lay in ambush
beyond light's reach
where whirring bugs
  drawn to the light
will soon cease
to whirr
in tightened jaws
        each bug
a chameleon's feast

then
in succeeding moments
almost
without notice
the real symphony
begins

with
night-bird cries
and ca-cawing lullabies
counter-point
to the syncopated dialogue
of several
hundred-thousand
flute-throated tree-frogs

who
whorrwip, whurrip, whorrip
through their
echoing, re-echoing
enharmonic songs
never over-lapping
near
    far, near
          far
until first-light
      dawns

ps
vive la noche
en Casa Terron
a donde paradiso
no es perdi
pero es hallo*

*Translation:
The night lives in
Terron House,
where paradise
is not lost,
   but is found

Emotion's Love and Like

EMOTION is hard put
to explain and answer questions
about her child, LOVE

LOVE is a very precocious child
and tries to behave and entertain
but she lets you down more often than not.

LOVE has had so many set backs
that I often wonder how she grows
and spans the distance between each Heart.

At first, when LOVE was still young
she stared about mystified
and included everyone.

Then as she grew older
she got to know her sister, LIKE
and they became such good friends.

LIKE guided LOVE; hand in hand they went
LIKE being older and more experienced
introduced LOVE to her first Heart.

LOVE was a novice
at the affairs of the Heart
but LIKE had known so many.

LIKE taught LOVE all she knew
about caring for her first Heart
being faithful, being warm.

LIKE was smart, but not as much as LOVE
for LOVE had so many more of the traits
of their Mother, EMOTION.

So LOVE took over and excitedly
she tried and tried to care
but alas, she broke her first Heart.

Her second Heart
came more easily than she thought
and she vowed to keep it with her forever.

Her second Heart was untrue
LOVE cried, but Hearts three, four, and five
came right along the very next day.

I gave my Heart to LOVE
somewhere down that numbered line
ah, but all of my Heart was not enough for her.

I have seen LIKE many times
since then
today, she asked me how long had it been

it was hard to tell her so
but the last time I saw LOVE
was some seven-hundred Hearts ago.

new leaves

turning over new-leaves
everyday
      one
            by
                  one
for a thousand years
only to find
in the early hours
of the morning's sun
      one side's wet
      the other
            crispy-dry

today
I think I'll wait
      till noon
and only pick up the leaves
           I know are done

Clair de lune II

~for my father: William H. Sadler, Jr.

from her hands the moonlight of Debussy still trickles
from her fingers and twinkles among the keys
love, you have seen me in the light, you have seen me
in the night where I shine through forest leaves
where I shine through transoms and under the eves

where I look out upon lawns slaked with silver toward
lonely trees whispering against the wind
casting hues darker than the night upon the lawn yet
caught comet-bright in mercurial highlight
can you see me

yes love as cloud passings uncloak the night, I see you
still in your beauty though less with sight
how could I not see you and all the moments we shared,
in all the moments as one.... we shared
you were always there - a love without compare
how could I not love you and all the moments we shared

shared even as the last ray of silver slipped from
between the leaves and from my fingers
now only echoes of you remain in my imagination
and in the notes you wrote our love still echoes
                    in musical refrain... it was fascination

and now as I hear the haunting lyric ode perpetuating
the memory of the moon,
of Claude Debussy, of you, most of all perpetuating you
love I see you still, in the musical magic of *Clair de lune*

Clair de Lune III

[for William Henry Sadler, Jr., my father]

Each fingered key sings its note of Debussy
On copperwire sweet-heartfelts strike destiny
The sound of memory ringing true and clear
The bittersweet perfumed kisses on your ear
The whispers of I love you, spoken so easily

Did you hear the music in my heart's fantasy
Its quick arpeggio played out slow and fancy
Our breath's tremolos when heaven was near
We are all instruments, and each of us sings

The piano my heart, the clarinet your *kami*
My words and your voice the perfect simile
Swords and sheaths, can both kill with fear
—and moons can drown in love's last tear
Clair play me quickly and I'll play you slowly
We are all instruments, and each of us sings

71

tree houses

December 21, 1990
winter's shortest day
in Sacramento
and a record cold wave

the jet stream
of super-chilled
arctic air
usually held captive
in Canada and Alaska

detoured through
the Sacramento valley
blew away
the tulle fog
in route
to other cities
further south

robust clouds
as ready reinforcements
marched in afterwards
with military precision
claiming total
air superiority
                in minutes

shades of victory
without a fight
snow clouds
basked in their
imitation darkness
leaving the sun
a mere
gauze defused
spot light

wary
birds of prey
flew only
out of necessity
from here to there
and only
on the wind
    not against it

for their
usual snacks
of still-plump
field mice and such
abandoned
their scavenger hunts
hours ago

and here
I am traveling
old cold backroads
like a fuller-brush-man
when I spied it
    without furniture
        or walls
just a skeleton
a mere silhouette
against the
    grey-light sky

there
naked and exposed
an abandoned
children's-home
reduced to a
seven-rung ladder
      leading to
a bare-plank platform
once carefully
nailed across
the now-wintered boughs
of a solitary tree

reminding me
of years ago
when lily tomlin
          as "edith-ann'
told of hiding
          tree houses
with successive
coats of paint

there's greens
for spring & summer
and reds
and golds and browns
to match the leaves
before
they-all-fall-down

then edith-ann
striking at the heart
          of the problem
of hiding tree houses
among the leaves
lamented:
but when winter comes
and all the leaves are
          gone
you have to move out!!...

and, obviously
that's the truth...
puffbphuffpbbbbbfbbbb!!!...

The St. John's Bay Collection Letter

your letter, postmarked yesterday
arrived at noon
in eager disappointment a blank page
        unfolded onto the clipping
           provided no clue

though the photograph was black and white
behind her [out of focus] clung
the azure confluence of sea and sky

the tropic sun drips kindly from over her shoulder
where her face, in sunshine's pale shadow, gathers
the light from her double-scoop white cotton tee
and the whiter Caribbean sand

the hip of a dune for a seat, she watched
           head turned
toward the source of her mostly enigmatic smile

the bottoms of her stretch twill Capri pants shade
each patella, while the lower half of her legs reach
toward the beach, toes scrunching the sand while
fingering bits of dune grass
        that stick up here and there
as
  though brush strokes on a artist's painted beach

for a moment I thought she might be saving that
smile for me—till my eyes caught the glinting gold
of her wedding band

remembering where I was
        I shook my head and turned the page
after all it was only a photograph
a women's-wear-fashion-advertisement with
golf equipment ads on the next page—no help

what clue, this—and disguised as a letter but
a letter without 'the letter', is only an envelope
and though a picture may be worth a lot of words
        I'd have rather had a letter
           ending with, I still love you

Letter: *So you're think'n' o' goin' to L.A.*

you won't hear any thunder in California
but the lightening, burns up the hills

you won't have to dodge any tornadoes
but the earthquakes can sneak up on you

they don't have any spring Blue Bonnets
but they have blue Lupines two feet tall

they don't have any Tex-Mex in California
so for that you'll just have to come home

they don't have Purple Martins or Cardinals
but they've got Blue Jays as big as Crows

there are more mountains and beaches
but the North Star won't look the same

most of all, on a starry night in California
you'll know, for sure, you're not
                    Deep In The Heart of Texas

Richard, I cannot go with you… Part I

beyond the rainy railway station
a grey and winter's day
greeted the marching Germans
        on the Champs Elysees
along with the keening knell
of silent churching bells
composed of dying notes in requiem
for fathers and brothers lost
who there in heaven wept
        as angels sighed

for the old men, the old women
the hidden younger mothers
and even younger daughters left behind
in whose minds was
the last hiding place of French pride

only they were left
to sing their blessed La Marseillaise
    ...Entedez-vous dans nos campagnes
    … Oh, do you hear there in our fields
    mugir ces feroces soldats?[1]
    the roar of these ferocious soldiers?
as the fleeing French
found themselves refugees again…
        Paris licked her wounds
        and the world cried
        God save Victor Laszlo

Richard, I cannot go with you… Part II

pacing the soggy train platform
planning their escape south
Rick waited for Ilsa in the rain
thinking the conductor could
    marry them on the train

at last Sam arrived
without Ilsa at his side
she was no where to be found
    … had *checked out*, Sam said
        and left this note behind

tearing open its envelope
    Rick's world changed in just
        seven quick lines
those inked lines of Ilsa's
the words, and their meaning
dissolved before Rick's eyes
in the splash of his tears
and the drizzle of the Paris rain

shouts of
aaalllll-aaaaboaaarrrd
    the railway conductors yell

as Sam and Rick jump on
Ilsa's crumpled note was tossed
       disappearing
into the engine's steam
that mixed with the Paris fog
as more tears from heaven
           fell

Richard, I cannot go with you… Part III

in the circumstance
of year-after-year of war
and the uncertainty of tomorrow
    love found today
like a single budding rose
    amidst the rubble of life
        is to be clung to
as if it is life's last sweet breath

surely no lover or autobiographer could
surely no diarist would
so surely only a novelist, a playwright
        or screenwriter could
have penned so painful a parting shot:

Richard, I cannot go with you or ever
see you again. You must not ask why.
Just believe that I love you. Go,
my darling and God Bless You. Ilsa[1]

and for no other reason than to
        advance the plot
the music swells and the scene dissolves

---

[1] the railway scene, Paris flashback, from the movie Casablanca ©
Warner Bros. 1942

L.B.A. to Rick's and *beyond*

Feeling harassed
heart kettle-drumming
like the big German guns
ba-boom-boom
        ba-boom-boom
raining fire
and spitting hell
at the hem of Paris

I dreamt of you
        again
and the way we were
before the Germans
      marched in

Though
that was another time
      another dream
      another war
        I've not forgotten
how the gun's muffled roar
severed my hand's grasp
  like Hamlet's sword slipping
    through the tapestry
    and poor Pelonius' cloak
from your tender heart
      and drowned out
        words of hope
leaving me the way I feel

Truth is chance meetings
rarely get second chances
to break fate's seal

And I've never been
     to Paris, or Rick's
but I'll keep looking for you
at La Belle Aurore
and all we shared
        before

letter postmarked Paris

the river ran chocolate with the loam
of cornfields not yet sprouted
   [no telling how many of thier seeds
  will germinate on Planter's Bar
                down river]

the rains have just this moment ceased
the weary, cloying clouds wrung clean,
           still cling closely overhead
holding to the tips of trees like a halo
  like wet fingers holding cotton-candy

my footprints stagger backwards across
the black skin of the field
      each step a further sticky-coating
           on my Wellington's
which now stand frozen-in-place where
I stepped out of them
to climb the ladder to my old tree-house
  once a freshly painted childhood refuge
now a very wrinkled face
that looks down and over a usually quiet
           and erubescent river

drying my hands in my coat's lining
I pull, from its inside pocket, your letter
[the one you wrote from Paris in 1967]
     careful to keep it out of the drips
          from the sieve-like roof

next I put on my reading glasses
[funny, I didn't need them
  way-back then to read your letter]
[funnier, I don't need them now as I could
     recite your letter from memory]
—I wanted to see again
        how you connected
the "o" to the "v" when you wrote in the
second line, *I don't love you any more*
      and compare it with

the "o" and "v" in the fifty-seventh line,
...there's a new love in my life, goodbye

I had gone to Vietnam,
which had been abandoned by the French
and you had gone to France to abandon me
—oh I know you didn't plan it that way
        who plans to fall in love
            in Paris
I'm sorry it just sort of happened, you wrote

it just sort of happens, *n'est-ce pas?*
              I've heard that too

I would have given anything to have been
with you in Paris, floating on the Seine
        not down the Mekong River
            with twenty un-tamed gorillas
                wearing tiger-camo's
drawing irregular green and black patterns
in grease paint across
           their Asian and American faces

by the time I got your letter
and read your news,
your new life in Paris had become a habit
one I knew an Illinois farm-boy
           could never break

I have carried that letter and the hurt
    [that hissed through my heart]
      that seeped deeply into my body
like blood spilled across a dirt hooch floor]

thirty-two years of remembering
what I thought was mine
what I thought I could only lose to death
        and death had spared us both

I looked again at the letters "o" and "v"
they seemed sad in the second line and
                    seemed satisfactorily happy
                            in line fifty-seven
it was just as I had remembered,
you seemed happy when you said goodbye…

your letter, now torn into pieces
        [one piece for each of the years
        I had kept it close to my heart]
floats on the black swollen river below me
its pieces
            floating
                    down river
                        [like the corn seed] to the
                    waiting fertile soil of Planter's Bar

who knows what
from the seeds of a *DearJohn* letter grows
but in that one simple act, I regained my heart
perhaps someday
                    something new there will grow

Homecoming Letter to Mom

Dear Mom

I'll be coming home soon, and can't wait to see you and River-Kitty
I don't know if you have read between the lines of my other letters
that there was or might be something else, something new in my life
but when I come home with a year of stories I'll also bring a wife

I know this is sudden to you, but in the loneliness of this last year
it could not have come too soon, no one could have done more, she's
one of the doctors in the hospital who treated me and saved my life
the wounds to my heart she stitched with her love, now she's my wife

I just couldn't face writing you, in fact for three weeks I couldn't write
and had one of the medics imitating my scrawl so you'd think I was ok
prepare yourself, I'll be somewhat handicapped for the rest of my life
& you always thought I'd marry an American, well I have an Asian wife

See you soon!

Chin-Wei Ti

Regret Letters: An Officer's Duty

yesterday when the sun rose over our hill
we knew by the clouds of black in the sky
that it was going to be a *wet-monkey-day*

the monkeys come down from the canopy
sometime after midmorning, at least that's
the way it appears, to those who notice

one old-grey-one seems to be the tribal
weatherman, coming out of the trees and
seemingly staring skyward counting clouds

most days, *dry-monkey-days*, it's everyone
for himself with the old-grey-one directing
traffic from the tall grass to the fruit trees

on monsoon days, *drowning-monkey-days*
he keeps everyone up in the thicker leaves
chattering: at least we're getting fresh water

on *wet-monkey-days* he gathers everyone
on a mound of grass and they make a sight
dancin' in the rain like they're taking a shower

Charlie only ever comes on *dry-monkey-days*
so we've developed a love-hate relationship
with our safe *wet* and *drowning-monkey-days*

the old-grey-one and his troupe had been
showering for about an hour when the first
mortars fell and Charlie breached the wire

the old-grey-one screamed as his clan ran
for the trees, but Sgt. Cox, your Tom never
heard him and I regret to have to inform you

we lost Tom and thirty-two of his company
today, good men all, and brave—not that it
counts except to those of us they protected

the-old-grey-one's shower-mound was only
five or six meters from Sgt. Cox's bunker
and when Sgt. Cox fell and Charlie advanced

the old-grey-one ran screaming toward Tom
beating his chest, bearing his fang-teeth; he
kept Charlie from reaching Sgt. Cox's body

when the fire-fight was over th' old-grey-one
lay dead, his back against Sgt. Cox's leg
his teeth and fangs still bared in a scary grin

it was clear to those of us who took notice
that the old-grey-one was protecting Tom
who prepared and left MRE's for him to eat

that was Sgt. Cox, always helping someone
or something, we all loved him in our way, but
even the old-grey-one couldn't help him today

and Mrs. Cox, it *was* the first *wet-monkey-day*
Charlie had attacked us, and Sgt. Tom Cox was
prepared, he just never got the chance to duck

the first mortar round took out his position
I'm so very sorry Mrs. Cox, Tom was the kind
of man we wanted to see ride the freedom bird

I am so very sorry Mrs. Cox, what can I say
this was just not supposed to happen, I know
yeah this is war, but it *was* a *wet-monkey-day*

counting the letters till you come home

my dearest darling I am so wonderfully
amazed that love
               so quickly consummated
has so long endured without you here
            not that I ever doubted our love
we had a lifetime—growing up together
            next door neighbors as it were
               then five days of courtship
                  after Pearl Harbor
                  and our two-day
                    honeymoon
perhaps it is that I keep my love alive
by pouring out my heart to you in letters
never knowing for sure
              if or when you'll get them
perhaps it is that little Nancy gets bigger
            everyday and she's never seen
            her Daddy, except in the two
            pictures from our wedding day
I am determined as is Mother Williams
for us to once again be a family
I say that only because when you return
it will be to us, not just me, but then
         we knew the war was coming
when we took our vows
       and knew that honeymoons often
            have certain results
since we have no way of counting days
till your return, we settle for counting
       the days you've been gone
and converting that to letters, one-a-day,
would you believe I've written you
one thousand and ninety-nine letters and
tonight's makes an even eleven hundred
we pray the war will be over soon
and with its end, you'll be coming safely home.
your loving Beatrice, Nancy & Mother Williams

p.s. we've been saving up our love for you;
our pennies, we save to buy more stamps.

Monday 1 June 70, Republic of Viet Nam
what was and *[wasn't said]*

Dear Mother, received your letter this morning
although it came in the mail yesterday
[the FNG mail clerk forgot to deliver it to me]

Yesterday I got my first day-off *[from the war]*
in—gosh, I can't remember when,
                            so I went with friends
                                to Red Beach in Da Nang
[rockets don't fall there, at least not lately]

We had a very good time, *[if you call six gimpy
soldiers splashin' one another and drinkin' beer
                                a good time]*
                    the ocean was a little
murky but quite refreshing, despite the brine
*[salt still stings in my wounds so I didn't get
all gunked-up with soap like the other guys]*

Needless to say the sun was quite hot and I got
a burn, my daily 'fun-in-the-sun' of about an hour
[walking the perimeter for physical therapy]
was not enough accumulated resistance to
                    withstand three hours on the beach
*[but who cares, nobody's getting toe-tagged
                    and body-bagged for sunburn]*
                            guess, I'll never learn

[but after all the jungle heat] boy nothing beats
standing in the cool ocean, waves lapping up on
                    you… and drinking an ice-cold beer
[unless I was back in the world, rockin' my girl]
                            —wow, that was good

Sorry to hear of Gary's set back, I hope more
can be done for him
                    Yes I got a letter from Becky
last week, so I got caught up on what all she
                            and Bob have been doing
[he's one lucky som-bitch, not havin' to be here]

88

Yes I did get the book you sent me. I am
really happy you are getting to make your trip
to Europe, I wish you a beautiful bon voyage,
             I know you'll love it
[thank God everything's okay, back in the world]

I am sending you a picture
   not a recent one *[that would be too scary]*
but one taken on 25 February 1970
             [before I got shot]

Love, A.J. *[I miss you mom, more than you
                   could ever guess]*

Title from a line in a letter from Sherry Sadler McDonnell *and*
["south to meet spring" —Leon Hale columnist *Houston Chronicle*
from a column 2-22-2000 *A journey to map spring's geography*]

I wonder if Spring's reached Brownsville?

for Sherry Sadler McDonnell, Leon Hale, & Morgan of Sweeny

Vermonters—never worry about spring
in Texas—they have to wait long enough
      on their own, but they do wonder

does it really freeze in south Texas—ask
any citrus farmer there…you'll get reports
      by year and billions of bushels lost

no, it's the citizenry of places like Houston
[where oil-duchy's of fur-wearers fly up to
New York to visit winter and their minks]

that get lonesome for spring in February
when the weather is as cold-nasty-bad
as Texans ever let it get

89

it's the spring-day dreamers
[who can't wait to shake that old
dis-enchantress that is winter's last day]

like Hale of Houston—Morgan of Sweeny
who conjure trips "south to meet spring"
so's a grim reaper can't steal their last'un

it's sharing: another year together; passing
another rite-of-passage; *Hale's Primavera*
his annul *Houston Chronicle* column sent to

her Brownsville father [who enjoyed it with
her] who loved to celebrate spring—sending
northern friends a single Texas Blue Bonnet

reminding them
they were not only missing out on spring
        but the beauty of spring in Texas
and it's sisters [missing their fathers] who
wonder if spring's reached Brownsville?

—if I had to guess
it must be close to spring in Brownsville
the "Snowbirds" have started driving North
and medial oleanders daily blush farther-up
the highway—inch by inch like a sunrise

no time for letters: a soldier's ticket home

no time for letters—hoping
to find the solution beneath the cloud of night
only to wake from those dreams without resolution
the soldier stared across the wasted broken ground

the dying soldiers' graves dug by the night-long rain
of mortar shells bursting, tearing through the earth
as if giant gardeners had just started
                        planting spring bulbs

the soldiers dying in place lay like scorched
and broken dolls
                akimbo
            some staring through open unseeing eyes
while the incarnate world around them swirled

midst the wails and moans
medics and litter bearers wheedled
as the occasional sniper's bullet sang
killing air if nothing more
                the sergeant screamed *move out*
                        get moving here
                                move out

then like thoughts that flash answers to the brain
the solution finally came
his ticket punched, the soldier marched on
                    cold then warm then serene
                    Jesus, Lord, hello
                    Hello son, welcome home

Reflections
on The Shawshank Redemption; Letter

from behind the thick brick
and masonry of prison walls
old Red walked free after forty years

found freedom had become the real prison
and outside fear made him dream of being
once again free 'inside' and free of fears

Red, but for Andy's promise made
would have shuffled off like Brooks
into another stream of life

the story's a metaphor for life's
new beginnings, Red in a red truck,
dusty back roads and corn-filled hills

Buxton's hayfields in the heat of July
true north [like friendship] at the end
of a compass needle Red finds the hill

it's Andy's old oak tree and rock wall
like one in a Robert Frost poem
that stands the tests of time

where weary mules bray
as the plow scratched Earth yields
the shoulder of another buried rock

from some of God's great ground
farmers gather rocks as much as
they prepare their field for crops

grunting lifting the farmer shoulders
to the stacking place
the latest furrow-stopping boulders

what was one by itself became two
then three together these fieldstones
placed one by and on another anon

until that stacking place became
a waist-high wall that stretched
o'er the hill like an ancient eyebrow

there it was at the end of the eyebrow
near where two lover's had lain
just like Andy said, the black Lucite rock

and digging down old Red found
the old tin box - its money envelope
and a letter that starts

Dear Red and ends, *hope is a good thing*
and good things never end
                    your good friend Andy

hope is a good thing Red found
when digging pays the bounty on
no walls at all and a ticket to ride

a bus bound for Texas borders
then south to a friendship in Zihuatenejo
and their freedom regaled by the sea o'

love letters from the sky

after you left and the promised phone calls didn't come
I'd check the mailbox perhaps four or five times a day
hoping each day for some note from you

just when the memory of our time together was fading,
after three lost years of waiting,
and I decided to give up hope of every hearing from you,
                    I got the news

you liked mystery (I suspect there were other reasons too)
so you'd never tell me just where you were from
and we'd only shared those eight days under the famous
blue Jamaica skies, anyway you said you'd call or write

I was ready fly to Canada, Montreal, Quebec or wherever
and bring you back to Texas as my bride
you said you'd never get over being rejected if *I* never called
even as I left you at the airport, with you insisting I not come in
you still would not give me your address and number
            while showing me you still had mine
                        anyway you said you'd call or write

I never knew what flight you took or the airline you were on
I just knew you were off to Canada to tie up loose ends
so the plane crash in Atlanta never caught my eye
though our separate flights increased the time and space apart
we were closer in the air that day than we would ever be again

after you left and the promised phone calls never came
I still checked the mail box perhaps four or five times a day
hoping against hope each day for some contact with you

just when the memory of our time together was fading,
after three lost years of waiting,
and me deciding to give up hope of every hearing from you,
                    I got the news

I received a letter on governmental letterhead
they were forwarding eight stamped letters that were
addressed to me
the government's letter said you were deceased

having died in the crash of flight one-oh-five
they'd held your effects: a flight bag with eight letters
and since they'd not found any next of kin they were
disposing of the flight bag and sending me the letters

for four days I kept company with the rain and cried
but on the fifth day your letters came
                                    and there wasn't a cloud in the sky

on your flight to Montreal you had written me eight letters
one for each day we'd been together
but before you got to Atlanta they fell with you from the sky
I know now, I was flying home to Texas the day you died

your eight letters were bundled in the hair ribbon
I had bought for you on the beach at Negril
untying the bundle each letter was marked: *I love you,*
and *open me 1st, 2nd, 3rd, and so on through 8th.*

now I knew the reason why
and once again I could take pleasure in
remembering our eight days and seven nights in love
for now I had received your letters, eight love letters
                              love letters
                                    that had
                                          fallen from
                                                the sky

[from Vol 5 Chp 3 Un-saved Odds and Ends pg 70]
Genesis of the novel: Jamaica Moon
– *from the Black Book Investigations of Michael Grant and Associates*

the domino letters

having told this tale till it needs no voice
    it tells itself
[even when a force is set against it]
as a kite against the breeze is held fast
    to sweetly kiss the wind's face
as long as it has one string's grasp on
        the earth

she and love, she and love become long
lines of shes and loves
    dominoes falling one upon
one and right after one another

life is the constant battle of standing up
all the dominoes
    knowing the fall, the slip
        is coming
    knowing that two must fall
      together and where
        two fall
          all fall

why
[given physics not to mention human
      nature] would he
want to fall in love again unless he knows
that only
    by standing up again does he stand
  a chance of being the last domino
    to fall on you

March Avenue Mulberry Trees
[letters from summer safaris of 1953]

1.

heat in the hundreds
grass, dry yellow-brown like wheat stubble
as parched as the sands of the Sahara
lay in the unfertile patches
[guarded by sidewalks and driveways]
        we called front yards
summer was yet to hit its stride in Texas
the heat of August still three months [away]
and the only reason we called it summertime
is yesterday 26 May—we got out of school
       for summer v-a-c-a-t-i-o-n

if springtime
cost a dollar-and-the-month-of-May
then the bill was already paid
      and there wouldn't be any change
August's heat was still three months [away]

awaking just after second bell, and realizing
this time I'd not be late for school my mouth
lifted up one little corner and waved a smile

today the summer safaris started
I would not try turning over and going back
to sleep this was after all the easiest day
of the year for getting out of bed
since—yesterday we got out of school
       for summer v-a-c-a-t-i-o-n

two bowls of Post-Toasties® and milk
saw me out the door and down to Jimmy's
who I learned was AWOL from my plans
    he'd been drafted and spirited away
      to camp with his aunt and uncle
        —summer-camp I learned
          lasted three weeks
          shy of forever

2.

peace had not yet been declared in Korea
the Armistice was two long months [away]
but the war March Avenue Mothers were
fighting was with a killer called Poliomyelitis
an insensitive dis-ease
　　that took kids off the playgrounds
　　　　　　　　　　in the middle of the day

the newsreel pictures of Iron Lung kids
[before the Saturday Matinee] had us
scared enough to mind maternal orders—
had us taking naps and getting hooked on
Search For Tomorrow & *The Guiding Light*
the Salk Vaccine was one long year [away]

3.

safaris started at dawn [seven to eight a.m.]
by striking-camp [getting out of bed]
and ended around four hours later with lunch
'cause we had to stop for rest-naps at noon
August's heat was still three months [away]
& o'course afternoons were too hot to safari

this morning's mid-morning heat rolled up your
arms and legs—while the sweat ran down
with Jimmy gone to camp *Cooler-In-The-Mountains*
got me to thinkin' where I might find a breeze
a little shade
　　then my mind [like a finger-pop] replied
　　　　　　　　　the Mulberry trees

past safaris had been spent in their branches
cradled above leaping leopards
[I didn't know then leopards loved to climb]
　　　　and hidin' from that roamin' red chow
with its scary slobberin' black mouth
the closest thing the neighborhood had to
　　　　　　　　a real tear-you-apart lion
paddlin' down the Mombosa [the Midlaner's

sidewalk—we called *the river* 'cause it was
always underwater when it rained
not that it was likely to rain till October] and
August's heat was still three months [away]
—oh yeah paddlin' down the Mombasa
was the only way to get
to the thick oasis-like Mulberry grove
[the single Mulberry tree] that grew beside
                    the Midlaner's garage

careful of the canyons, the deep fissures
in the black gumbo land of Dallas that heat
and no rain caused
last week [before school let-out] Jimmy lost
two companies of army-men down the crack
                    of one of them
two days of diggin' —still hadn't found 'em
tomorrow they'd be declared missin' in action
so the letters home wouldn't sound so bad—

mindful of the canyons, I made it to the tree
and began to climb [careful this time,
yellowjackets also like the Mulberry's shade]
into its boughs, beneath sticky viscous leaves
and onto the garage roof [so steep-pitched
balls always rolled right off-it] luckily I had
trusty well-worn safari shoes
            [black high-top PF Flyers®]
                    which held me like glue to the
                        grit and tar-paper shingles

            4.

the morning breeze was more convection
hot-air rising up under a leaf-dark canopy
but it felt good like a happy birthday smile
its thickness kept almost all but the tiniest
shards of sunlight that filtered through
[to focus like rays in a magnifying glass]
into little spots here and there on the roof
        one spotlighting a row of ants traversing
        the channel between some broken shingles

99

it was a place of infinite daydreams—was the
closest I ever came to visions of sugar plums
dancin' above my head
                    'cause when I'd open my eyes
I'd see Mulberry clusters all within arms reach
in a chameleon cornucopia of colors
small bitter green ones, those turning pink, the
just-red, the riper-red, and the blue-black ripest
—and I had eaten them all
today I only picked the ripest, eating enough to
make it possible for a growin' boy to miss lunch
                              and not miss it

knowing your territory is imperative and I knew
mine—when the shadows of the telephone poles
crept close to their creosote feet it was time
            I had to run quick for home
I could miss lunch, but not nap-time—
had no hankerin' to be *swallured* by an Iron Lung
with the heat of August still three months [away]

I never thought about it, the evidence, not once,
till I'd get to my front door—then out of breath
memory'd scream *wipe your mouth…*
ops too late—fingers already covered, shirt
and lips bloody with the heady juice of Mulberries

my past explanations of bloody leopard encounters
were countered with irrefutable mother-knowledge
such as *there are no leopards on March Avenue*
and I wouldn't admit to being scared
   of being chased again by that mean ol' red chow
chased up-into the most convenient Mulberry tree
so I'd accept my admonishment
—*thought I told you not to be eatin' those berries*

my only retort—the only retort
of polite southern boys in the nineteen fifties was
                    a [bashful head-down] *Yes Ma'am*

maybe tomorrow I'll go on a bone-safari
to the local La Brea tar pits
[the asphalt street a block away] where
[we'd sometimes find stuck-up dragonflies]
the afternoon heat blew tar bubbles in the street
that were great fun to jump on
listening to them explode under your feet
tho' it meant a detour to the gas station
[before going home] standin' in a pool of gasoline,
we'd drip outta the nozzle—
that usually would take off most of the tar
    'least enough that after walkin' home
none would be comin' off on Mom's linoleum floors
that dried off faster'n than Mom could mop 'em
though the heat of August was three months [away]

it was 27 May 1953
peace had not yet been declared in Korea
the Armistice there was two long months [away]
it might as well have been summer in Dallas
but the heat of August was three months [away]
Jimmy's big sister had gone off to another camp
to live in an Iron Lung
—Jonas Salk's vaccine was one long year [away]

Dallas Museum of Art

in preview
from Musee' d'Orsay
came
Monet's
stripe-spangled
rue Montorgueil
        with flags
and Cezanne's
Strangled Woman

to stir
the artist within
to set at cusp
anew
the hunger
to create
with pigmented oils
similar visions
held
in mind's lock

impressions
of colors waving
of darkness bright
and light subdued
    in contrast
one
with the other

as with Cezanne
presenting
a limbo
of light and shade
creating
a crescendo
of power
its balance
                lost:

the strangler
    imbalanced
with unseen
darkened grip
wrests
from his victim
her earthly powers

shown released
at that moment
of lost consciousness
with her arms
beginning to
           fall
              away
their struggle failed

and with Monet
creating his illusions
of opacity
with translucent
strokes of color
    gossamer reds
     veils of blue
   and whites of
almost every hue

my passions
usually spent
awash
in less creative
tides

find inducement
to conjure
that element
long not used
to issue forth
those impressions
I know
each blank canvas
hides

Lament For PEGASUS RED

With the warmth
of the summer night about us
we walked the downtown Dallas streets
in the early nineteen fifties

I guess I was only four or five
for my arm was stretched
way above my head
to clasp my Dad's hand
and I had to look straight up
when he pointed to the place
where the buildings end
      and the sky begins

Look, he urged,
    look at the Flying Red Horse!

I laid my head back
steadying myself against his leg
and stared at the sky

I remember being confused
at not seeing the object
pointed out
      except
for my mind's vision
of a flying red horse
    jumping
from building top
  top building top
galloping across the sky

As kids are inclined to do
    to please my Dad
I said I saw the Flying Red Horse
after
    asking where it was again

Some summers later,
as the Republic Bank's tower
    [R.B.T. we called it]
stood head and shoulders
above the Mercantile
                and its clocks,
the kids on March Avenue
gathered atop
a neighborhood garage
for their nightly meeting

While watching the RBT,
    its neon lights alternating
        white, then blue
        then white, then blue
    the steady long red strip
        on its side
    and for mesmerizing fascination
    RBT's crowning searchlight
        went probing
                sweeping
    the summer darkness
two kids questioned the rumor
that the weather could be foretold
by understanding the changing
of the tower's colored lights
        and I
was retelling the story
    to the new kids on the block
how my Dad and I
had first seen the Flying Red Horse
[that of course, I didn't really see]

Over the years
as Dallas and I grew
the Flying Red Horse
remained
    instead of the North Star
    or Orion's Belt
my celestial starting point
and a welcoming beacon
    of friendship

each time I returned home
from outland adventures

Now, on tonight's returning
there will be
no more majestic red glow
coursing through
Pegasus' outlined veins
[for progressive City Ordinances leave]
only a darkened
Magnolia Building landmark
    standing mute
against the skyline
of future children's dreams

Lament For *PEGASUS RED II*
de nova

City sign ordinances siphoned from our sight Magnolia's light
and Federal policies dampened a thousand lesser lights

so much so that during the darkening of the Carter-years
friendly home-town beacons became a memory to travelers
who often found their own porch-lights their only welcome home

happily, entrenched darkness did not last and in the skyline
of future children's dreams, mine and theirs, it came to pass

when in the early 1980's Dallas City Fathers once again
threw the switch and gave our Flying Red Horse a new
neon infusion

for a while longer with unobstructed view Pegasus watched
and guided millions and millions of Texas Lone Star travelers
providing these weary crusaders with a Big D welcome home

some years and progress later... now corralled by even taller
building peaks, whose backsides and bellies bask in old Red's
    glow
old travelers such as I, with practiced eyes, can still catch a
glimpse, in passing, of their favorite red horse on the fly

however, from tonight anon when trip-weary children wake
to ask: are we there, yet—though miles away, they'll see
another majestic sight etched into the Dallas Sky

the InterFirst Tower, the new guiding light, its edges
of argon green passionately outlined against the night

their touchstone seen, their haven nearly reached, they feel
safe again, as did I, and fall back, fast asleep
into Technicolor scenes [mine were red—theirs are green]
of this the Dallas skyline of future children's dreams

Lament For PEGASUS RED III

Joyous was his birth, out of Medusa, beauty's claim
and where'er touched Pegasus' hooves in Dallas,
there sprang loyalty, gathering all hearts who saw him,
a fixture steadfastly poised; a comfort to the Muses.

by new millenium's red light

the interurban nexus of connecting highways
draws travelers like darts to its Dallas center
where a landmark, a beloved terran lighthouse,
calls home its ships safely from its sea of streets

the armada's ships, emblazoned with epic names:
Packard, Ford, Studebaker, Olds, and Chevrolet
Buick, Cadillac, DeSoto, Plymouth, and Mercury

gave birth to future ships: the Grand Marquis,
Voyager, Cougar, Windstar, and Coup de Ville,
Impala, Corvette, Firebird, F-150 and 500 SEL

past & present ships, their Captains and crew, all
found comfort in the crimson-lighted leaping steed
whose purchase secure, since nineteen thirty-four,
now finds himself, rusted like a tin-man in the rain,
awaiting the lighting of
                    the new millenium's resurrection

as if from Medusa's head to spring again
                    the flying red Pegasus will
                    a constellation reborn in metal
            with newly armored coat of porcelain
        and a rosy transfusion in his glassy veins
    resume his turns upon the Dallas skyline's stage
        of still more future children's dreams

	Poem	Page			Poem	Page

and other selected poems

other books

Novels by

Robert J. Sadler

Jamaica Moon
Judas Oracle

both
available through
your local bookseller
createspace.com
amazon.com

Author's website:
robertjsadler.com

published
by
wordsculptorpress

Made in the USA
Charleston, SC
08 May 2010